Presented to

From

On this date

Sisters by Birth

Friends by Choice:

ALL THE THINGS
I LOVE ABOUT YOU

BY ELLYN SANNA

A DayMaker Greeting Book

You are my Sister...

and you are far more

for you are one of my closest friends.

What's more, you are—

and always have been!—

one of my very favorite people.

So many things make you who you are. . .

and I love them all!

Sister...

Friend

I love your friendship...

For there is no friend like a sister

In calm or stormy weather;

To cheer one on the tedious way,

To fetch one if one goes astray,

To lift one if one totters down,

To strengthen whilst one stands.

—CHRISTINA ROSETTI

Friends can come and go with the changing circumstances of life. But no matter where life may pull us, the bond between you and me always holds. Through all life's sunny summers and stormy winters, I count on you. Your constant friendship gives me strength. That's why I love you!

Sisters—they share the agony and the exhilaration. As youngsters they may share Popsicles, chewing gum, hair dryers, and bedrooms. When they grow up, they share confidences, careers, and children....

— ROXANNE BROWN

Over the years, you and I have shared so many things.

What would my life have been without you?

Who would I have been without your love and friendship?

I'm so glad God made us sisters!

The desire to be and have a sister is a primitive and profound one that...is a desire to know and be known by someone who shares blood and body, history and dreams, common ground and the unknown adventures of the future, darkest secrets, and the glassiest beads of truth....

—Elizabeth Fishel

In thee my soul shall own combined
The sister and the friend.

—Catherine Killigrew

When I talk with you, I see myself a little clearer—not the dressed-up, made-up me I wear in public but the me I take into God's presence, snarls and bags and crabby streaks and all. Thank you for accepting me just the way I am.

You are one of the best friends I've ever had.

In a world that's unpredictable. . .often frightening. . . sometimes overwhelming, I'm so glad I can count on your friendship.

We'd fall asleep holding onto each other's hair.
—ASHLEY JUDD, about her sister Wynonna

Harmony

I love the way
we get along...

You are just like me.

You are nothing like me.

Both things are true.

And in the tension between

those opposite truths,

God blesses us.

A sister can be seen as someone who is

both ourselves and very much not ourselves—

a special kind of double.

—TONI A. H. MCNARON

Learning to share wasn't much fun when we were young.

But you helped me understand that when I give to you,

I am blessed. The more I share, the more God gives to me.

One of the best things about being an adult is

the realization that you can share with your sister

and still have plenty for yourself.

—BETSY COHEN

I think if there's no sibling rivalry in a family,

there's a lot of denial going on,

because you can't help but rub against each other

when you're forming who you are.

— JOANNA KERNS

Growing up, sometimes we couldn't help but rub on each other's nerves. After all, we shared a table. . . the back seat of the car. . .a bathroom!

Today, we have more space between us, and we don't rub each other the wrong way as often.

Grating against each other's rough spots may have been painful for us both.

But I know that same loving friction helped shape the women we are today. In the end, even our fights have blessed me!

Children of the same mother do not always agree.

—NIGERIAN PROVERB

When we were younger, sometimes I'd dress like you, do my hair like yours, try out the things you enjoyed. Then other times, I'd do anything just to be different from you. I didn't want our teachers or our parents or anyone else to mistake me for you. I wanted to be my own person, not your duplicate. Now that we're older, once in a while I still have those old feelings.

But most of the time, I'm more comfortable with myself. I don't have to fight so hard to prove I'm as good as you. Instead, I'm grateful we're so much alike. I love you because you understand me so well. Just don't borrow my favorite sweater, okay?

A sister is both your mirror and your opposite.

—ELIZABETH FISHEL

Sister is probably the most

competitive relationship within the family,

but once the sisters are grown,

it becomes the strongest relationship.

—MARGARET MEAD

You and I are tied together by years

of misunderstandings. . .

cross words. . .

icy silences. . .

laughter. . .

hugs. . .

tenderness. . .

and love.

All those strands are twisted into a knot

that nothing will ever, ever break.

Love is patient, love is kind.

It does not envy, it does not boast,

it is not proud. It is not rude,

it is not self-seeking,

it is not easily angered,

it keeps no record of wrongs. . . .

It always protects, always trusts,

always hopes, always perseveres.

Love never fails.

— 1 Corinthians 13:4–5, 7–8

Sisterhood is to friendship

what an arranged marriage is to romance.

You are thrown together for life,

no questions asked (until later),

no chance of escape.

And you, if you're lucky, you find love

despite the confinement.

—LISA GRUNWALD

I didn't choose you.

You didn't choose me.

God simply threw us together.

I'm so glad!

Gratitude

I love all the things
you have done for me...

All our lives, I've watched you shine.

You've made my own life brighter

with your light.

If one life shines, the life next to it will catch the light.

— ANONYMOUS

Advances toward heroism in her sister

made Elinor feel equal to anything herself.

— JANE AUSTEN, *Sense and Sensibility*

When I watch you tackle a hard job,

I'm proud of you. . .and I take heart.

If you can do it, I tell myself, then so can I!

I love you for putting your hand into my heaped-up heart

and passing over all the foolish and frivolous

and weak things that you can't help dimly seeing there,

and for drawing out into the light

all the beautiful radiant belongings

that no one else had looked quite far enough to find.

— ROY CROFT

Thank you for bringing out the best in me.

The Bible says angels are God's messengers, the bright, winged beings who bring God's love to those of us on earth. You may not have wings, or a halo of shiny gold, but you still fit the description, for all my life you have been there, showing me God's unconditional love. You've helped me see His face a little more clearly.

That's why I love you!

A ministering angel shall my sister be.

—SHAKESPEARE

You and I learned about life together. . .

how to get along with boys. . .

how to get along with our parents. . .

how to get along with each other!

But the most important thing I learned

from you was how to get along with God.

My sister. . .was the one who showed me

what women of faith look like.

She taught me how to live.

—CAROLINE BURNS

So many times you and I have shared a table, a hot drink, something sweet to eat, heartaches, and laughter. Those moments are timeless spaces of contentment and comfort, moments that hearten and encourage, that give us both strength for our days. You're such a good friend —and that's why I love you!

Two people sitting over a pot of tea and hot
buttered teacakes push all the huge international
anxieties to the edges of perception—
and live for a little while in an Eden of their own.

—Pamela Dugdale

There can be no situation in life
in which the conversation of my dear sister
will not administer some comfort to me.

—LADY MARY WORTLEY MONTAGU

Sharing my life with you is one of my life's
truest comforts—a little like putting tired,
pinched feet into warm, soft slippers.
No matter what happens to me, I always know
it won't seem so bad once I've talked with you.

To fall down you manage alone,
but it takes loving hands to get up.

—YIDDISH PROVERB

When life knocks me flat, I have tendency to want to lie there on my back and wail. But you always reach down, give me your hand, and help me up. Then you dry my tears, hug me, and make me laugh again.

That's why I love you!

You may not know all the times you've rescued me. Sometimes it was just your smile, your voice on the phone, just the familiarity of your presence.

But just by being you, you made my life seem better.

I'm so glad we're sisters!

It's just the little homely things,

The unobtrusive, friendly things,

The "Won't-you-let-me-help you" things. . .

That make the world seem bright.

— AUTHOR UNKNOWN

Life is not made up of great sacrifices

and duties but of little things:

in which smiles and kindness given habitually

are what win and preserve the heart

and secure comfort.

— SIR HUMPHREY DAVY

Thank you for your loving habits. You are such a comfort to me. (Maybe that's why I love you so much!)

Maybe I could have gotten along in life without borrowing your clothes when we were young...without trying out your makeup...without spraying your perfume behind my ears.

And maybe I could have survived without all the times since then that you've helped me in big and little ways.

But it wouldn't have been much fun.

When we can share—

that is the poetry in the prose of life.

—SIGMUND FREUD

There is no desire so deep as the simple desire

for companionship.

—GRAHAM GREENE

You know why I love you?

Because you're always there

(even when "there" is the end of a phone line);

you always care;

I always know you understand.

As long as you're in the world,

I'll never be all alone.

Yes, there is a talkability

that can express itself even without words.

There is an exchange of thought and feeling

which is happy alike in speech and silence.

It is quietness pervaded with friendship.

—HENRY VAN DYKE

Sisters experience something that others may not understand, a connection that is deeper than words.

It's almost like a secret code, a private language that only they share.

Thank you for sharing with me the secret language of your heart. Thank you for being not only my sister but my friend.

Wishes and Prayers

Then give
to the world

the best you know

And the best will come back to you.

—Henry Wadsworth Longfellow

I swear to you there are divine things
more beautiful than words can tell.

— WALT WHITMAN

Because I love you, I long for you to have life's best.

For most of my life I've been watching you. You may not always choose exactly the same paths to follow that I do, but whatever road you take, you always give your all.

Even when I was young, you inspired me to do my best...simply because you always did. That's one of the things I love about you.

I pray that God always give you His very best.

Long ago, you and I took our first steps, first you, then me; first me, then you.

Today, we each have our own pace, our own stride. But along the way, you've showed me that life can be more than just plodding along, one foot in front of the other. You taught me to listen for life's music. . .and you showed me how to dance.

May you always hear life's music, and never forget to dance.

If you can walk, you can dance.

If you can talk, you can sing.

— ZIMBABWE PROVERB

I love the way you help me see the brighter side of life. In if ever your own life seems dull. . . discouraging. . . even bleak, I'm always here, wishing you joy, praying you'll catch a glimpse of divine delight.

The sun, with all those planets revolving around it and dependent on it, can still ripen a bunch of grapes as if it had nothing else in the universe to do.

— GALILEO

I know how busy your life is. . .so many people and things are dependent on your skills. I'm proud of you, more than I can say. . .but today, I wish for you time to smile, time to simply feel the sun on your face and the wind in your hair.

May you find time to bask in God's presence. Soak up a moment of eternity. Take time to ripen your soul.

Imagine the two little girls we used to be. Do you think they would recognize the women we've grown to be? We've come so far.

I love you for all the years we've shared. . . and who knows where God will lead us next?

May you never settle for living up to less than your true abilities.

And may you be astounded and delighted by all God has in store for you.

If we did all the things we are capable of doing,
we would literally astound ourselves.

—THOMAS EDISON

Forever

I love knowing you'll always be there. . .forever!

Only you remember that special Christmas. . .

that awful birthday. . .

the wonderful jokes. . .

the terrible fights. . .

the laughter. . .

the tears. . .

the hugs. . .

the taste of home.

No one else can understand the way

you do and always will.

I guess that's why I love you so much!

No matter where I travel, home is always as close as

the nearest phone and the sound of your voice.

Your Siblings

are the only people in the world

who know what it's like to be

brought up the way you were.

— BETSY COHEN

Even when [my sister and I] are separated

by continents, we are moving through

time in parallel tracks.

—KENNEDY FRASER

For any weaving that needs to be done,

God sends the threads.

—ITALIAN PROVERB

Ever since we were children, God has woven our lives together. When I look back, I'm so grateful for the part you've played in my life's tapestry.

As I look ahead, anticipating the pattern of the years to come, I'm glad for the constant strands of your love.

Whatever you do. . .

they are connected to you till you die.

You can be boring and tedious with sisters,

whereas you have to put on a good face with friends.

—DEBORAH MOGGACH

No matter what my hair looks like. . .

how much weight I gain or lose. . .

or the size of my bank account,

you'll always be my sister.

What good news!

Can you imagine being old women together. . .

looking back on all the years, still laughing, still sharing?

I bet when we're old,

I'll love you even more!

What a wretched lot of old shriveled creatures

we shall be by-and-by.

Never mind—the uglier we get in the eyes of others,

the lovelier we shall be to each other.

— GEORGE ELIOT

Often, in old age, they become each other's

chosen and most happy companions.

In addition to their shared memories of childhood

and of their relationship to each other's children,

they share memories. . .that carry the echo

of their mother's voice.

— MARGARET MEAD

I love you now

I'll love you later.

I loved you then.

I'm so glad we have each other

to share our memories.

Is the world all grown up?

Is childhood dead?

Or is there not in the bosom of the wisest and the best,

some of the child's heart left? . . .

—CHARLES LAMB

Some days I feel so grown-up.

Not in a good way, but in a tired, worn-out way.

Then you and I get together, and we start to giggle

over some old memory, some familiar joke. . .

and suddenly, I'm a child again.

That's why I love you!

Heirlooms we don't have in our family. But stories we've got.

—ROSE CHERNIN

*Y*ou and I share things in common, but more than ordinary friendship keeps us close year after year.

I know what your toes look like curling in the sand beside the ocean; I remember the way your hair waves behind your ears; I know the shape of your hands, your nose, your smile, almost better than I know my own.

And no matter how many changes time brings, I will always know. I will always remember.

I can imagine some day in eternity, when the saints will look up and see a new bright, shining being.

"Who's that?" they'll murmur. But I'll see past the glory of eternity to a face that will still be as familiar as my own. "That's my sister," I'll answer, as I hurry up to greet you.

All our lives, we've taken turns breaking the path ahead for each other. I follow in your footsteps; you follow in mine. When it's my turn to blaze the path, I like knowing that you are close behind.

When it's my turn to follow, I'm always comforted to know that someone so beloved and strong has come this way before me.

And then there are the times, when we walk side by side, sharing the adventures together.

You help me not fear the future.

I'm so grateful for your presence in my life. Seeing you is like going home, in the truest sense of the word. I feel secure, safe, sheltered, just as I did in the happiest moments of my childhood.

Your presence is one of the places in my life where I can say, "Here I am safe. Here I can be myself. Here I am loved."

How vast a memory has Love!

—ALEXANDER POPE

Thank you, sister,

for being my friend.

I love You!

DayMaker
GREETING BOOKS

© 2003 by Barbour Publishing, Inc.

ISBN 1-58660-819-3

Cover Image © Daryl Benson/Masterfile
Book design by Kevin Keller | designconcepts

All Scripture quotations, unless otherwise indicated, are taken from the
HOLY BIBLE, NEW INTERNATIONAL VERSION®. NIV®. Copyright © 1973, 1978, 1984
by International Bible Society. Used by permission of Zondervan
Publishing House. All rights reserved.

Published by Barbour Publishing, Inc.,
P.O. Box 719, Uhrichsville, Ohio 44683. www.barbourbooks.com

Member of the
Evangelical Christian
Publishers Association

Printed in China.

5 4 3 2 1